5/2013
ACPL Laramie, WY
39092083442626
Hamilton, John,
Stock cars /

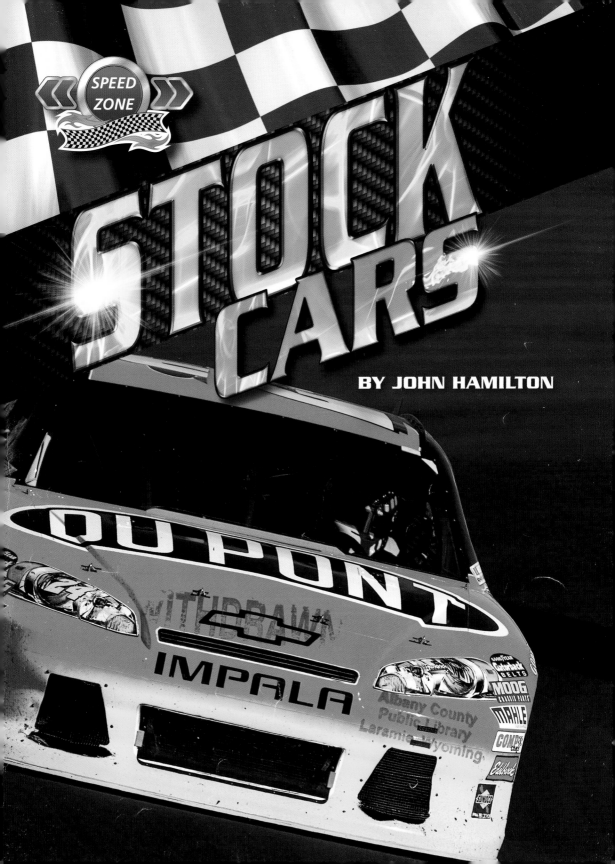

SPEED ZONE

STOCK CARS

BY JOHN HAMILTON

VISIT US AT
WWW.ABDOPUBLISHING.COM

Published by ABDO Publishing Company, PO Box 398166, Minneapolis, MN 55439. Copyright ©2013 by Abdo Consulting Group, Inc. International copyrights reserved in all countries. No part of this book may be reproduced in any form without written permission from the publisher. A&D Xtreme™ is a trademark and logo of ABDO Publishing Company.

Printed in the United States of America, North Mankato, Minnesota.
052012
092012

 PRINTED ON RECYCLED PAPER

Editor: Sue Hamilton
Graphic Design: Sue Hamilton
Cover Design: John Hamilton
Cover Photo: Corbis
Interior Photos: Alamy-pgs 12-13 & 16; AP-pgs 9, 20-21, 22-23, 28, 29; Corbis-pgs 1, 4-5, 10-11 & 30-31; Getty Images-pgs 6, 7, 8, 14-15, 18-19 & 24-25; Goodyear-pg 17; iStockphoto-pg 32; Thinkstock-pgs 1 (Speed Zone graphic) & 2-3, United States Army-pgs 26-27.

ABDO Booklinks
Web sites about racing vehicles are featured on our Book Links pages. These links are routinely monitored and updated to provide the most current information available. Web site: www.abdopublishing.com

Library of Congress Cataloging-in-Publication Data

Hamilton, John, 1959-
   Stock cars / John Hamilton.
      p. cm. -- (Speed zone)
   Includes index.
   ISBN 978-1-61783-531-5
   1. Stock cars (Automobiles)--Juvenile literature. I. Title.
   TL236.28.H54 2013
   629.228--dc23
                        2012012689

CONTENTS

STOCK CARS

Stock car racing is one of the most popular motorsports today. Stock cars resemble regular street cars, but they are built for racing.

XTREME FACT - Headlight-shaped decals are placed on the front of the body. NASCAR vehicles don't have real headlights.

There are hundreds of dirt tracks and asphalt raceways across the country. Each week, stock cars bump and draft for position, often mere inches apart, at speeds close to 200 miles per hour (322 kph). Stock car racing is a thrilling spectacle.

HISTORY

In the 1920s and 1930s, mass-produced cars became affordable for the public to own. Some people enjoyed racing these "stock" cars. Many races were held on the beaches of Florida. People also raced on dirt tracks in Southern states such as North Carolina.

Street cars perform a pre-race run at Daytona Beach, Florida, in 1936.

XTREME FACT - During Prohibition, people who illegally transported liquor were called bootleggers. They drove fast, modified cars to evade police. Some later competed in stock car races.

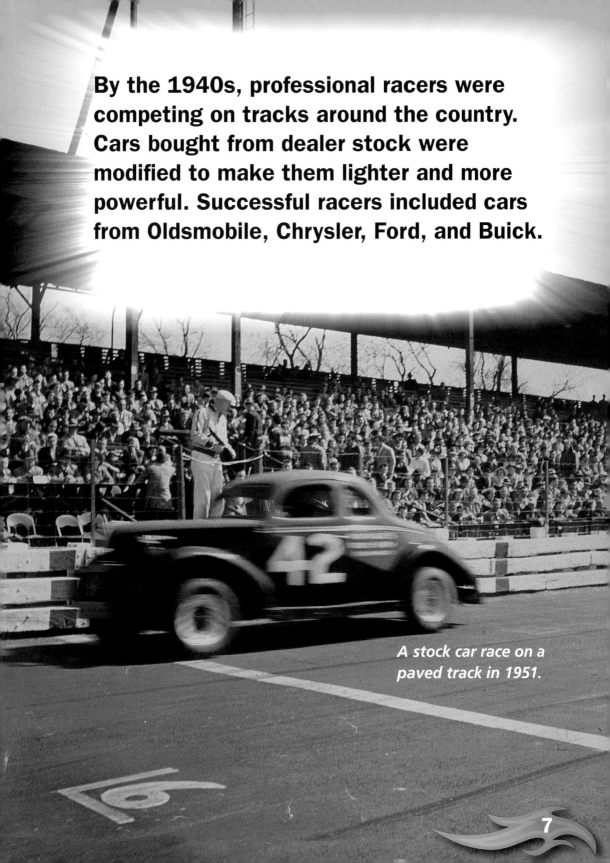

By the 1940s, professional racers were competing on tracks around the country. Cars bought from dealer stock were modified to make them lighter and more powerful. Successful racers included cars from Oldsmobile, Chrysler, Ford, and Buick.

A stock car race on a paved track in 1951.

NASCAR

In 1948, race car driver Bill France Sr. formed the National Association for Stock Car Auto Racing (NASCAR). He wanted stock car races to be fair. NASCAR organized rules and regulations.

Bill France Sr. at the Daytona International Speedway in Daytona Beach, Florida, in 1959.

XTREME FACT - *Today, most NASCAR teams maintain from 12 to 20 stock cars at a time, with annual budgets of more than $20 million.*

Today, NASCAR oversees the largest and most popular racing series in the world. These include the top-level Sprint Cup Series, the Nationwide Series, and the Camping World Truck Series. The 2012 Sprint Cup Series includes 36 races held on several tracks over a 10-month period.

The checkered flag signals the winner of a NASCAR Sprint Cup Series auto race at Dover International Speedway in Dover, Delaware, in October 2011.

RACETRACKS

Stock cars race counterclockwise on oval or tri-oval tracks. There are usually three or four turns. Steep banks make it easier for cars to take turns at high speed.

The Talladega Superspeedway is a tri-oval. This term describes the track's combination of shapes: a triangle and an oval.

The Talladega Superspeedway, near Talladega, Alabama, is the longest track in the United States. It measures 2.66 miles (4.28 km) per lap. The famous Daytona 500 is a 500-mile (805-km) race held at Daytona International Speedway in Daytona Beach, Florida.

FRAME AND BODY

Even though they are called stock cars, today's **NASCAR** vehicles are heavily modified race cars. Teams must follow strict guidelines.

Stock car frames, called chassis, are made of steel tubing. The driver's compartment is called the roll cage. Stock car bodies are handmade from sections of bent and shaped sheet metal. They are welded together and attached to the frame. Afterwards, the car is painted and decals are applied.

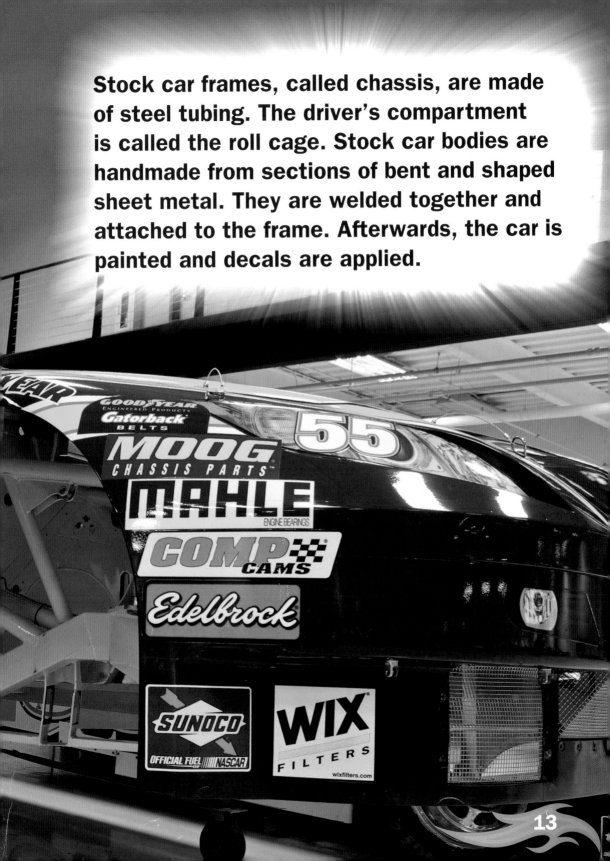

ENGINES

NASCAR engines have eight cylinders. Starting in the 2012 Sprint Cup season, NASCAR engines use fuel injection instead of carburetors. Advanced electronics and sensors in fuel injectors make the engines run more efficiently. NASCAR teams build their own engines. The engines can take more than 100 hours to build. They cost between $45,000 and $80,000 each. Strict regulations must be met when building engines.

NASCAR engines can produce about 750 horsepower. Unrestricted, they can propel the cars at speeds of more than 200 miles per hour (322 kph).

SUSPENSION AND TIRES

A car's suspension system connects the wheels to the frame. It includes springs, shock absorbers, and linkages. In stock car racers, the tension of the springs is very important. Springs absorb energy. They help keep the tires in constant contact with the track.

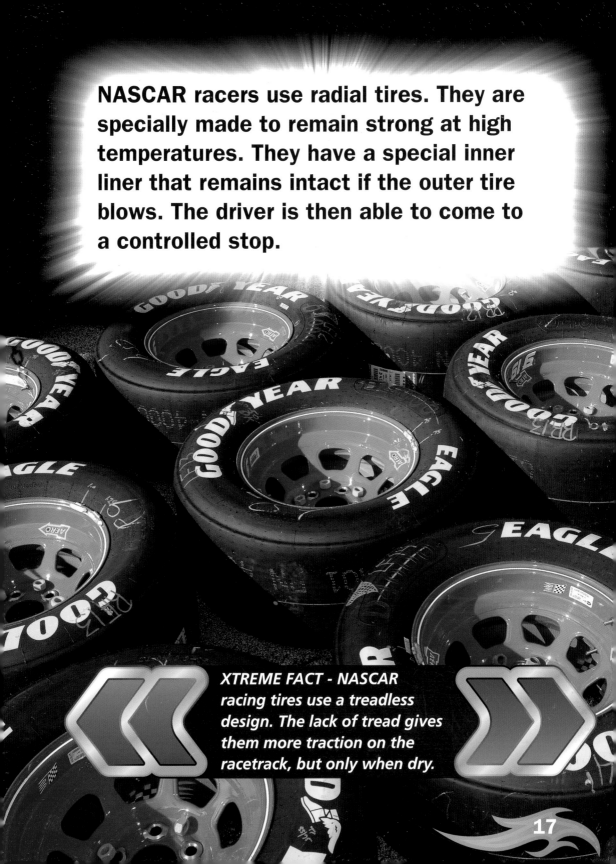

NASCAR racers use radial tires. They are specially made to remain strong at high temperatures. They have a special inner liner that remains intact if the outer tire blows. The driver is then able to come to a controlled stop.

XTREME FACT - NASCAR racing tires use a treadless design. The lack of tread gives them more traction on the racetrack, but only when dry.

THE COCKPIT

The cockpit is where the stock car driver sits. In addition to the steering wheel and gearshift, the cockpit is filled with controls, gauges, and switches. The driver constantly monitors the car's performance.

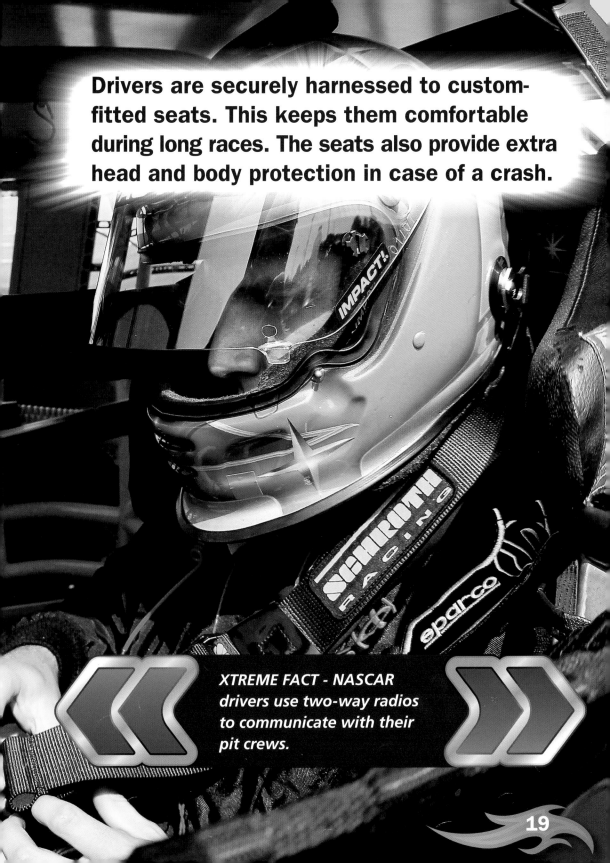

Drivers are securely harnessed to custom-fitted seats. This keeps them comfortable during long races. The seats also provide extra head and body protection in case of a crash.

XTREME FACT - NASCAR drivers use two-way radios to communicate with their pit crews.

SAFEGUARDS

NASCAR is constantly rewriting the rule book to keep drivers and spectators as safe as possible. In the recent past, stock cars became too fast and powerful. Deadly crashes resulted. NASCAR now uses restrictor plates. These engine devices limit a car's top speed to about 190 miles per hour (306 kph) on superspeedways.

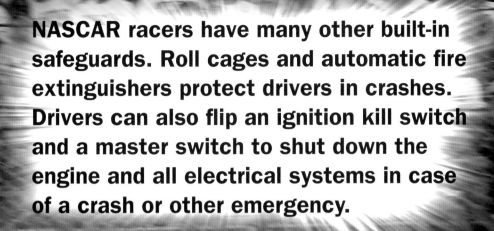

NASCAR racers have many other built-in safeguards. Roll cages and automatic fire extinguishers protect drivers in crashes. Drivers can also flip an ignition kill switch and a master switch to shut down the engine and all electrical systems in case of a crash or other emergency.

Carl Edwards goes airborne after being hit by another driver on the last lap of an April 26, 2009, NASCAR race. Edwards survived the crash. Safety is an ongoing concern for everyone involved in racing.

XTREME FACT - Window netting on the driver's side window keeps the driver's head and arms inside the car during a crash.

RACE STRATEGY

Forty-three stock cars compete in NASCAR races. It's like a traffic jam that moves at 190 miles per hour (306 kph)!

XTREME FACT - A 500-mile (805-km) NASCAR race takes about four hours to complete. A checkered flag is waved when the lead car crosses the finish line.

In this high-speed match, competitors often race very close to each other. Drivers have to know when to pass. They have to know how fast to take turns. Sometimes cars bump and grind against each other as they fight for the best position.

Cars are jammed together at the start of a NASCAR auto race at Charlotte Motor Speedway in Concord, North Carolina, in 2011.

DRAFTING

Sometimes the distance between cars is extremely close. Mere inches may separate the vehicles. This bold driving technique is called drafting. Aerodynamics is the way air streams over and around vehicles. Because of the way stock cars are shaped, at high speeds they "hug" the road.

When a second car trails close behind, both cars benefit from their combined aerodynamics. They may gain precious speed. Successful drafting is often the difference between winning a race and defeat.

XTREME FACT - Sometimes a drafting line, or drafting pack, will form. Three, four, or even five cars can form a line. The entire pack moves faster around the track.

PIT STOPS

During a stock car race, cars need to stop to refuel and change tires. A skilled NASCAR pit crew can perform these tasks in less than 15 seconds.

The United States Army pit crew races to change tires.

Seven pit crew members are usually allowed "over the wall." Each one has a special job. The gas man fills the car with large cans of fuel. A jackman uses a hydraulic jack to the raise the car. Tire changers replace tires using air-powered impact wrenches.

DRIVERS

Successful NASCAR drivers spend many years developing racing skills. They are also very physically fit, with enough stamina to endure a 500-mile (805-km) race lasting four hours. Drivers also need a good education to understand today's high-tech stock cars.

Jimmie Johnson

XTREME FACT - Many drivers get their start on dirt tracks. There are more than 800 dirt tracks across the country.

NASCAR has produced many famous champions in its history. Some of today's top drivers include Jimmie Johnson, Dale Earnhardt Jr., Kyle Busch, Jeff Gordon, Tony Stewart, and Danica Patrick.

Kyle Busch

Dale Earnhardt Jr.

Danica Patrick

Jeff Gordon

Tony Stewart

GLOSSARY

Aerodynamic

Something that has a shape that reduces the drag, or resistance, of air moving across its surface. Racing cars that have aerodynamic shapes can go faster because they don't have to push as hard to get through the air.

Carburetor

A device used in engines that mixes air with a fine spray of gasoline. Carburetors use suction to draw the gasoline into the cylinder.

Chassis

The body or frame of a vehicle.

Fuel Injection

A system that mixes air and a fine spray of gasoline into an engine cylinder. Instead of using suction to draw in the gasoline, like a carburetor, fuel injection uses a small nozzle to spray gas under pressure directly into the cylinder. Fuel injection has been widely used

on production automobiles for more than 30 years. It is generally more efficient than a carburetor, and saves gas.

Horsepower

Horsepower is a unit of measure of power. The term was originally invented to compare the power output by a steam engine with that of an average draft horse.

Radial Tires

Modern tires are made of a network of steel, polyester, or other textile material arranged in cords, combined with layers of rubber. In radial tires, the cords are wrapped at 90-degree angles from the tire's center, and are crisscrossed over each other. The cords give the tire strength.

Tri-Oval Track

A racetrack with three wide turns. The most famous NASCAR tri-oval tracks include the Talladega Superspeedway, near Talladega, Alabama, and Daytona International Speedway in Daytona Beach, Florida.

INDEX